Presented to

_____

From

_____

Date

_____

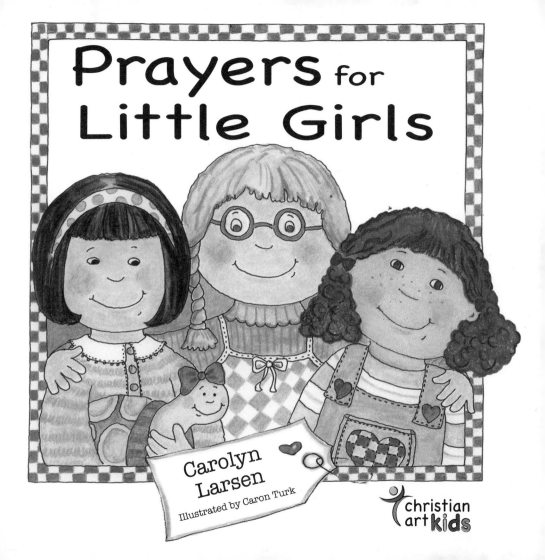

Prayers for Little Girls

Carolyn
Larsen

Illustrated by Caron Turk

christian
art kids

Praising God

Dear God,

It must have been fun to make
everything in the world! How did
You think of butterflies and starfish?
My favorite things You made are
flowers – red ones, yellow ones
and purple ones. Flowers smell nice.
They are pretty. I'm glad You thought
of flowers and butterflies and ...
everything!

Amen

Dear God,

You love me! I know You do because the Bible tells me so. You love me deeper than the ocean, higher than the stars ... more than anything! It makes me feel really special to know that You love me that much. I love You, too!

Amen

10

Dear Father,

Sometimes I don't act very nice.

Sometimes I'm even kind of mean.

But, when I tell You that I'm sorry,

You always forgive me.

Thank You for forgiving me and

always giving me another chance!

                              Amen

"I know the plans I have for you", declares the Lord,

"plans to prosper you and not to harm you,

plans to give you hope and a future."

Jeremiah 29:11

Dear God,

Nothing ever surprises You because You know everything that's going to happen. I could never have a surprise party for You. That's OK, though, because since You know everything, I don't worry about anything happening that You can't take care of.

That's a good feeling!

Amen

13

Dear God,

There was a thunderstorm last night. The wind made the trees bend all the way over. It rained so hard that we couldn't see across the street. Thunder crashed and lightning flashed. It was kind of scary until my mom said that the storm was showing us only a little bit of Your power! Wow!

Amen

Dear Father,

I like knowing that I can talk
to You anytime I want to.
You are with me here at home,
when I go to Grandma's house
and when we go on vacation.
You are everywhere! I like that.

Amen

Dear God,

Guess what? I love You!
I love You for making the world
and for making puppies and kittens.
I love You for giving me
my family and friends.
Most of all I love You for
just being You!

Amen

You can help me be brave!

Dear God,

Sometimes I get scared about things.
Like when I started pre-school or
when we went to a new church.
I know I can ask You to help me be
brave ... and You will!
I like that.

Amen

Dear God,

I was wondering ... do You ever get
tired of listening to my prayers?
Do You get tired of watching out
for all of the people on earth?
I know You never do because You
love all of us.
Thank You for always paying attention
and for watching over me all the time.
That makes me feel safe.

Amen

24

Dear Father,

Yahoo! I feel so happy today.

Know why? Just because of You!

When I look at big tall trees,

I think of You.

When I see tiny red flowers,

I think of You.

Birds flying across the sky and

worms crawling on the ground

all remind me of You!

Thank You for everything You made!

Amen

Dear God,

If I crawled down inside the deepest cave, could You still see me?

If I hid in the deepest, darkest forest, would You know where I was? You would! You can always see me. I'm glad!

Amen

27

28

Dear God,

You must want me to know all about You because You gave me the Bible. I like all the stories about people who followed You and how You took care of them.

My favorite story is the one about David and Goliath.

Thank You for the Bible.

Amen

Dear Father,

You love me today and You
will love me tomorrow.
You take care of me today
and You will take care of me
tomorrow and the day after
that and the day after that.
You will never get tired of loving me.
Thank You for always being the same.

Amen

Dear God,

You made the mountains and oceans.

You created butterflies

and pine trees.

Rainbows, lightning and seahorses

are all made by You.

You are amazing!

The most amazing thing is that You

are never too busy to think about

Dear God,

Know what I just thought of?
I'm talking to You right now and
clear over on the other side of the
world, in some place like Australia,
another little girl might be talking
to You right now, too.
You can hear both of us and You
care about both of us.
That makes me feel warm and
friendly about that girl in Australia.
Cool!

Amen

Thanking God

Dear God,

Thank You for thinking of families. I know my family loves me – even when I fight with my brothers and sisters or disobey my parents.

They love me no matter what.

I love them, too!

Thanks for giving me the perfect family.

Amen

Dear God,

Rainbows are one of my favorite things. A rainbow seems to cheer up the sky after a big thunderstorm. Thank You for thinking of making the pretty colors stretch across the sky. Rainbows remind me that You love me and take care of me.

I love rainbows!

Amen

42

Dear God,

I have the best grandma in the whole world! She makes cookies for me and pushes me on the swing. She tells me stories about when Mom was a little girl.
Thank You for my grandma. I love her!

Amen

Dear God,

Thank You for my friends.

Having friends makes everything more fun.

We play and laugh and sing.

Sometimes we put on shows for our moms and dads.

Friends are fun.

Amen

Dear God,

My daddy reads me stories from Your book every night before I go to bed.
My favorite story is about when Baby Jesus was born.
You must love us a lot to send Your Son to earth.
I love You, too.
Thank You for sending Jesus.

Amen

Mary and Joseph thanked God for Baby Jesus.

They knew that He was a very special baby.

48

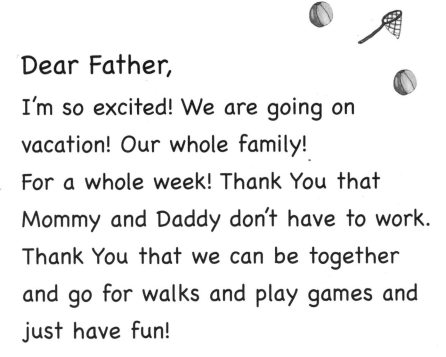

Dear Father,

I'm so excited! We are going on vacation! Our whole family! For a whole week! Thank You that Mommy and Daddy don't have to work. Thank You that we can be together and go for walks and play games and just have fun!

Amen

50

Dear God,

It's spring! The trees have tiny leaves on them and flowers are pushing up through the ground. I saw a robin in the yard and worms crawling in the grass. I love spring!
Thank You for thinking of it.

Amen

Dear God,

I'm kind of sad right now.
I was thinking about Jesus dying
on the cross. I am sad that
happened to Him when He loved
people so much.
Thank You for loving us and for
sending Jesus.
You must love me a lot!

Amen

54

Dear God,

I love my mom so much!
She plays with me and reads to me.
She sings silly songs and makes me
laugh. She takes care of me when I
don't feel good. Sometimes we make a
tent out of blankets and we sit inside
it and eat chocolate chip cookies and
marshmallows. My mom is great!
Thank You for my mom.

Amen

Happy Birthday to you ...

Pin the tail on the Donkey

Dear God,

IT'S MY BIRTHDAY! I have waited and waited for it. It took a long time to get here! I'm going to have a party today and all my friends will be here. We will play games and have cake and ice cream ... and presents!
Thank You for birthdays!

Amen

58

Dear God,

Know what? My daddy bought me
a puppy. He is white and brown
and really soft. His name is Buddy.
He gives me kisses and he plays
tug-of-war with a rope.
I love Buddy.
I think he is going to be my
best friend.
Thank You for my puppy.

Amen

Jesus ♥ You

Jesus is born
Luke 2:1-20

Love the Lord your God with all your heart, soul and strength.

Deuteronomy 6:5

Thank You, Jesus ...

Dear God,

Thank You for my Sunday school teacher. She teaches us lessons about You.

We make fun things in Sunday school and we learn verses from the Bible.

We pray for people, too.

I think my Sunday school teacher must be a lot like You.

Amen

Dear God,

I'm sorry ... again.

I try so hard not to be mean
to my brother, but sometimes
I am anyway.

I wish I was nicer.

Thank You for forgiving me
over and over and over.

I'm glad You do.

 Amen

Dear God,

Thank You for my mom and dad.

They work so hard to take care
of me.

They have jobs to earn money
and they clean the house and
cook the food and do the laundry.

I really love my mom and dad.

Amen

God makes cool stuff!

Dear God,

Thank You for butterflies and
ladybugs and fuzzy worms
and roly-poly bugs.
Thank You for bluebirds and geese
and hummingbirds and seahorses
and dolphins and whales.
You thought of so many things
for us to see.
Thank You for thinking of them all!

Amen

Saying I'm Sorry

Dear God,

My friend and I were playing a
game and I got really mad at her.
I yelled at her and threw the
game pieces at her.
Now I'm sorry. I really like her
and I want us to be friends again.
Help me be brave enough to tell
her I'm sorry.
Thank You.

Amen

Dear Father,

Sometimes I don't like to go to church. I do want to learn about You, but sometimes I just want to play with my friends instead of listening or singing or praying.
I'm sorry when I'm grumpy about church.
Please forgive me.

Amen

Dear Lord,

I did something bad. I told a lie to my mom. I was afraid that if I told her what I really did she would be mad at me.

Now I know she will be mad when she finds out I lied. I'm sorry for lying. Please forgive me and please help me be brave enough to tell my mom the truth.

Amen

Dear God,

I'm scared of thunderstorms.

I don't like the thunder and lightning.

Mom says I don't have to be afraid

because You will take care of me.

But, I'm kind of afraid anyway.

Please help me to trust You more.

Amen

Dear Father,

I promised my dad that I would clean up my room today. When he got home from work and saw my messy room, he was really sad because I didn't do what I said I would.

Please forgive me for breaking my promise and please help Dad forgive me, too.

Amen

Dear Lord,

I was playing at my friend's house today. We had so much fun playing with these tiny dolls she has. I really liked them. In fact, I liked them so much that I took one home with me. I just put it in my pocket and brought it home. I'm sorry for taking something that does not belong to me. Help me be brave enough to give it back to her and help me to never steal anything again.

Amen

Dear God,

Why do I have to brush my teeth every day? My mom keeps on telling me to brush my teeth all the time and I keep saying no.

She is unhappy with me and I am unhappy with her. I guess my mom knows what's best for me. Help me to just obey her without arguing.

Amen

Dear God,

We just got new neighbors. They have a little girl who is about my age.

I should be happy to have a new friend, but I don't like her. I know that isn't nice. She probably misses her friends from where she used to live. Help me to be nice to her. Help me to be her friend.

Amen

Dear Father,

I feel grumpy today.

I don't know why.

But I don't like being grumpy.

Please help me to be nice.

Amen

Dear God,

I keep making the same mistakes over and over. Mom says I shouldn't get upset, 'cause I'm still learning and growing.

I'm sorry that I sometimes learn slowly. Thank You for being patient with me.

Amen

Dear God,

I don't know why I did it. I sneaked into my sister's room and just messed it up. I dumped books on the floor and pulled clothes out of the drawers. I made an awful mess. She was really mad. It was a really mean thing to do. Please forgive me and help my sister to forgive me, too.

Amen

Dear God,

I cheated. I was playing a game with my brother and I wanted to win so I cheated. He always wins and I just wanted to win once!

But, it's not much fun to win that way. Please forgive me and please help me not to do that anymore. I don't like how it feels.

Amen

94

Dear God,

I'm jealous of my friend.

She has a new puppy and I want
one so much.

It's hard to be nice to her when
all she talks about is her puppy.

Please help me to stop being jealous.

Help me to be happy for my friend.

Amen

Dear God,

Sometimes I hear people say Your name in a bad way. That makes me sad because I know that's not a nice thing to do.

Please help me remember that Your name is special, because You are special. Help me to show I love You by saying Your name in nice ways.

Amen

Dear Father,

Sometimes I just don't want
to pray.
I wonder if You really hear
my prayers or care about what
I pray for.
Please help me to trust
You more and help me to keep
praying and believing that
You hear me.

Amen

Asking for Help

Dear God,

My grandpa is really sick.

I'm scared that he might not get well.

I really love my grandpa. He lets me

help him paint birdhouses and work

in his garden. Please take really good

care of my grandpa 'cause he is really

special!

Amen

Dear Father,

My friend is moving far away.

She is sad to leave her friends here.

I'm going to miss her a lot.

Help her make friends in her
new town.

Help her to like her new home a lot.

But don't let her forget me.

Amen

Dear God,

There was a really bad flood in another part of the world.

I saw on TV that people lost their homes. Lots of people died, too. Some children don't have moms and dads anymore and some children died. It's really sad. Help those people, God. Take care of them and help them to know that You love them.

Amen

Grandma & Me

Dear Father,

My grandma has cancer.

She is really tired and doesn't feel like playing with me anymore.

I miss her being the way she used to be.

Help the doctors know what to do to help her feel better and get well.

I love my grandma.

Amen

Dear God,

My daddy takes long trips
for his work.
He rides on airplanes and he goes
far away. Please keep him safe
while he is traveling.
Bring him back home to me
really soon!

Amen

Dear God,

I don't feel good.

My nose is stuffy.

My head hurts.

My throat is scratchy, too.

I guess I'm sick.

I don't like being sick.

It's not fun.

Please help me get better quickly.

Amen

Dear Father,

I got into a big fight with my friend today.

She yelled at me and I yelled at her.

Now we aren't talking to each other.

Please help us to make up.

I miss her.

I don't like to fight with my friend.

Amen

Dear Lord,

Sometimes I'm not so good at obeying Mom and Dad. When they ask me to do something I get grumpy and sometimes I even talk back.

Please help me to be better at obeying. It's so hard 'cause someone is always telling me what to do.

I really need Your help.

Amen

Dear God,

My brother is going to the hospital
today to have an operation.
He is kind of scared about it.
Please take really good care of him.
Sometimes I fight with him,
but I really love him.
Help him to be brave
and to get well soon.

Amen

Dear Father,

It is really cold and snowy tonight.
There are some people who don't
have warm homes to be in.
Please take care of them.
Help them to find some place
to go where it is warm and dry.

Amen

Dear God,

Why do there have to be wars?
On TV I saw people crying because
someone they loved was hurt.
Why can't people stop fighting?
Why can't they talk about what
makes them so angry?
Please help the wars to stop.

Amen

124

Dear God,

I want a puppy. My mom said,
"Maybe." Please help her to
think about it really hard.
I would take good care of my puppy.
I would play with him and take him
for walks and feed him and give
him baths.
Please help her to think about it
really hard.

Amen

Dear Father,

I don't mean to but sometimes I say mean things. Especially when I get mad at someone.

I feel bad when someone says mean things to me. I don't want to make other people feel bad.

Please help me to stop saying things that hurt people's feelings.

Amen

Dear God,

My mom is so busy. She works
hard and she is tired a lot.
Sometimes she is too tired to
play with me or read to me.
Please take care of Mom.
Keep her healthy and ... help her to
have time to play with me sometimes.

Amen

Dear Father,

My friend's daddy died. She is really sad 'cause she misses him a lot. I want to help her, but I don't know how. Please help her know that it's okay to be sad. And God, please take good care of her and her mom.

Amen

Now write your own prayer.

Dear God,

_____

_____

_____

_____

Amen